Punish the Elephant

Caution:

"The views expressed in this book are solely those of the author. Readers are advised to approach the content with critical thinking and to consider their own perspectives. Your understanding and interpretation of the material are at your own risk."

Copyright © 2024

All rights reserved.

ISBN:

Dedication

This book is dedicated to the young men and women who struggle with relationships. I wrote this book with you in mind. We have failed you as a culture. It is my hope that this book will bring you Hope.

Acknowledgment

My decision to write this book have a lot to do with the dynamics of me growing up as well as watching the brokenness in relationships from a little hill till now. I acknowledge all of those who have came into my life and brought the knowledge, agitation, frustration, disbelief that I needed at that time. To my mother, pops, my brothers, cowboy, my daughters, and my sisters, Christine Jame, Sherry and of course Grace. But mostly to God. Who gave me the information and allowed me the time to put it on paper. May he forever be glorified. Amen

Table of Contents

Dedication 4

Acknowledgment 5

About the Author 8

Chapter 1 10

    Is this you???? 10

Chapter 2 11

    The big lie.... 11

Chapter 3 14

    No man is going to tell me what to do! 14

Chapter 4 17

    Let's go back 17

Chapter 5 19

    Words and actions: 19

Chapter 6 25

    CONFLICT AND CONFLICT RESOLUTION 25

Chapter 7 29

    Authority in your relationships 29

Chapter 8: 32

    THREE FORMS OF AUTHORITY 32

Chapter 9 35

    Independent or interdependent? 35

Chapter 10 42

For the men....... 42

CHAPTER 11 47

Professional business woman/A wife (soft girl) needed 47

Chapter 12: 50

The Ring, the Paper, and the Vow 50

Chapter 13 53

The Four Roles of Family 53

Chapter 14 59

BRIDGES 59

Chapter 15 63

THE BOND 63

About the Author

The author of this book was born in Louisiana and raised in California. Growing up, the majority of his life was spent being somewhat defiant and confused. He is the oldest of three boys and one girl, with the girl being the youngest.

Originally, the author's household consisted of his mother and father, but something happened between the two that led to their separation. This caused the author to witness firsthand the dynamics of a troubled relationship. He later observed the dance of power between his mother and stepfather, which taught him about challenges that can arise in relationships.

Despite growing up in a two-parent home, the author did not graduate high school. Instead, he went to prison, having originally wanted to join the military. After the prison experience, the author went to college but had to leave when his beloved mother passed away around the age of 53.

Grieving the loss of his mother, the author threw himself into his work. It was his mother who had encouraged the author to write, recognizing his impressive abilities demonstrated through the letters the author had written to her while in prison.

The author later moved from California to Tennessee, still searching for his place in life. It was during a conversation with his then-girlfriend, who was not listening to the author's thoughts and experiences, that the author decided to put pen to paper and write this book, heeding his mother's wise words about his writing abilities.

The author's life experiences, including the challenges and insights gained from observing the relationships around him, have all contributed to the creation of this book, which the author hopes will provide solutions and assistance to those seeking to navigate the complexities of relationships. Especially the youth! I the author believe in this book. I gave it my all!

Chapter 1

Is this you????

I once saw a drawing of A beautiful woman. This woman was so amazingly beautiful. She was stunning. I tell you the truth, she was the type of woman that men write beautiful poems about.

Her smile, wow! Her amazing smile! It left me breathless. I took a step back and completely visually consumed her entirely. I noticed Her lovely womanly curves. Everything in its right place. She had the figure of what we men call fertile. Truly a magnificently built woman.

While staring at her more intensively, I noticed something. It appears that she has two left hands. Yes, two left hands. Sadder yet, one of her left hands (the one that would be the right hand) were deformed, twisted in on itself. Facing outward opposite of the healthier left. I felt sad, very sad for her, as I walk away knowing she would not be treated fairly or be given the same opportunity as a woman with two healthy hands. Even tho she is above average beauty. I know deep down most guys would probably pass her by and sadly settle for lesser Beauty than to have to deal with that deformation.

PUNISH THE ELEPHANT

Chapter 2

The big lie....

I can't begin to say how unbelievable this statement has been consistently pressed against my ears. Wow! I have heard it repeatedly throughout this society. There have been times that I wondered when the person mentioned this lie to me, whether or not they were truly aware of what they were saying. It sounds like one of those ridiculous statements that people pick up from other people and then just repeat it without thinking. To say that I was shocked would only be an understatement, the first few times I've heard it. After the initial shock, of course, I recognize that the reality is, there are people who actually believe what they were saying.

To say that the statements were cute or funny would not give them their true justice, nor will it express the deep-seated disillusionment and confusion to which it has been accepted throughout our entire society.

Categorizing the statement. It is a broken, sad idea at the very least and a perverted viewpoint at its best. Leaving no room for the prolonged healing that is so desperately needed. Closing the door on the one thing, yes, the one thing we desperately need the most in this country.

By now, you are probably wondering what I'm talking about???... Well, let me hold you in suspense no longer. What I'm speaking of is the idea that a smart, highly educated woman can be a man and a woman at the same time. Or, as its put, being a father and mother of a child at the same time. This is feminist psychobabble.

As anyone with a brain knows, that is impossible. Even our common definition of hermaphrodite has one set of reproduction organs, Amiss, the two genitalia.

I am well aware that this will offend some of my lovely sisters on this planet. I'm not attempting to offend. That's not my objective. I just want them to be truly empowered. Not a financial scapegoat for a society that capitalizes off their pain and family brokenness.

You did not pick up this book to be told the same old lie that has led you down repeatedly the wrong road again. You picked up this book to be told the truth. Only to be led to finally positive results. Long term relationships, get your money's worth. Part of being able to share with you the opportunity to receive the results that you most desperately treasure and desired is to be clear on a few issues and or titles.

We have for so long allowed the media and those that controlled the media to determine what we consider normal, fair, right, just, and good. The problem with that ideology is the media only shows what is popular that brings in the money. We know deep down that the media has no interest in ensuring that our family stay together. That is our responsibility. You could die right now; the Media wouldn't even stop to mention your name. But your family would be crushed for life. The media is only interested in making money. It's not personal. Therefore, you should not use its information personally. It is entertainment at its best, misinformation at his worst.

I don't know about you, but I am so tired of watching family lives broken. Precious, innocent children cry while Daddy walks away, not understanding why his marriage is falling to pieces. My heart breaks, tears fall down my eyes watching well-intended, honest, loving women are stripped of the marriage they believed in from the time they were little girl. Doing everything they were told by society and still coming up short or lacking. Not fair!! It's just simply not fair! Another woman screaming in deep, unconsolable confusion and pain as she surprisingly receive divorce papers from the man she has been with for 40 years. Good, solid women losing everything because they believed in something that initially and originally was intended for them. They believed in something bigger than themselves; they believed in family. My hope with this book is that not another woman will cry, be broken, or hatefully use the words, **I DON'T NEED A MAN**, because of the misinformation that was given to her by the media or a trusted friend/relative or stranger who subscribed to the same broken self-perpetuating trauma.

There is a formula, a real formula, that works and has continued to work for hundreds of thousands of years. Getting back to family forces us to take a good look at how far we have come as a society. We had it good for a while, but now things aren't looking relationally so good.

Most of us believe what the mainstream has told us. A great portion of the time we don't even question it at all anymore. Add the subconscious messages of those we love reverberating the same thing. We find ourselves walking towards those goals that were shaped by all types of conscience and unconscious messages. None of those messages help us to see **THE ELEPHANT IN THE LIVING ROOM.** We continually overlook the things that we need to address the most.

Instead, we are so super distracted looking the other way as we are being robbed of the most important thing on this Earth: Family. Don't you think it's time someone, anyone, mentions the void in our homes? Do you know where this Elephant came from? Can't anyone smell anything anymore? Have we gotten so comfortable with the scent of broken families that we act as if it's not there? Are you tired of moving as if everything is ok when you know it isn't.? Let's stop pretending! You were created for something much better than this. You only have one life. Every day, you're getting closer to the grave. There is an Elephant in the living room of our lives. Let's deal with it already!!!!!

PUNISH THE ELEPHANT

Chapter 3

No man is going to tell me what to do!

I promise to tell the truth, the whole truth, and nothing but the truth to help my sisters on this planet.

Submission/submitting to your mate! Ladies, before you tune out, at least listen to what I have to say. Please, I promise you it will change your relationship. I'm sure there are many opinions about this subject everywhere. It just depends on who you talk to and how close they are to you, whether you value what they say. As for me, here's the deal. Most women, from what I have learned, have an idea of what they want in their relationships. Most women have known for a long time what they want from a little girl until now. Many women have not been able to get anything close to what they have envisioned. The problem is making their partner see their vision. Well, ladies, it's much easier than you think. We live in a society that stress getting a job or career if you are a woman. You women hear it from everywhere. The media, within your community, and amongst your own family. To add to that is the pressure to find the right person/soulmate to marry and have a decent life. There seem to be no balance. If you're good at work, your love life is usually lacking/suffering or non-existing. If you're fantastic in your relationship, chances are you can't keep a steady job. With today's working women, the pressure gets more intense as the years pass to find that special someone. Let's face it, ladies, no one wants to be old and alone.

I do believe I have a new solution to your problem. Yet, I have an old solution to your new problem. Let's look at this word "submission". I have heard it from women I know, they say, "I don't want to submit; he will think I'm weak. Or only weak women submit to a man!" I took a real hard look at those statements and perspectives. Ladies, let me first say that I understand where you may be coming from with those types of statements. It's understood. Especially if there has been abuse in your childhood or adulthood, I get it. However, submitting is not a bad thing under normal circumstances. I'll prove it. When you go to the doctor, you submit to that doctor; when you go to the courthouse to pay a ticket or get pulled over by an officer, you're submitting. Each time you stop at a red light, you are submitting. As you can see you are constantly submitting in one way or another. Yet when it comes to this good man (notice I said good man), you won't submit to the things he is trying get you to see. **Here's the secret.....men can't fight humility (period). Men cannot fight humility.** Men can and will fight pride every day for years, but men can't fight humility. Humility is like kryptonite to a man. Humility is only weakness to a boy. Stop and think for a second. Before you were a woman, you were a little girl. You tell me what men did when they were confronted by your girlish humility?

I'm sure you have heard all the horror stories as I have about women who have been abused by boys posing as men. Or maybe you are one of those abused women. The sad part about these stories you don't hear is how they got that way. You only hear about the women that were abused. I'm not going to deny that there are men (boys who appear to be men) who abuse women. Everyone knows that. What I'm saying is that there is more to the story than what we hear. Let me say it this way: when men and women get together, they are usually on their best behavior. No male (boy) is going to let women know that he is an abuser. Nor is any woman going to tell a man that she will confront him and argue with him repeatedly, sometimes for no real reason. Many males have self-esteem issues that are rarely addressed. That is a different conversation for a later day.

It is believed that males are strong, and this is true in regard to physical strength. However, physical strength is not an issue in this topic. Emotional and mental strength is. When it comes to those areas, women have more strength, hands down.

Men talk a good game, but women live it better. Men are people. They are human, and they Hurt. Even though some men act as if they don't feel any pain, in reality, they actually do. We are all subject just to the human experience. We all have the human condition. We all hurt, get sad feel cheated, feel misunderstood, been laughed at. We have all dealt with life as life happens before our eyes. To believe that one human being on this planet does not have fear or pain is a bold face lie.

I have yet to see any quiet women get choked- D. L. Hugley.

It's true any woman who is humble towards her man stands a great chance of never having many problems with him. The reason why that is its because Men can't fight humility. I know the media tell women a different story. But look at the facts. 79% of marriages crash land in divorce court within the first 5 years today. Yet, we continue to believe in the media's version of the roles we have as men and women. Really, why?

Insanity is doing the same thing and expecting a different result.

Someone comes to you today and says, I'm going to give you a house. It is perfect, and it's all you ever wanted. But it's 79% broken or 79% missing! You're seriously not going to question that? Even though you watch and see other people go through the exact same thing in their lives and how their lives are shattered. Are you seriously going to mimic/do the exact same thing to get the exact same outcome? Are you foolish enough to believe that you are special, that you somehow have the formula to develop a great long-term relationship, when other people who think and act as you do don't? I have been sharing this information for years. The people who use it stay together. Those who don't don't. It's that simple.

PUNISH THE ELEPHANT

Chapter 4

Let's go back.......

In a previous chapter, we discussed abuse. However, we did not go into detail regarding domestic violence, nor did we discuss low self-esteem amongst men.

It has been my experience throughout this time on this earth; I have seen multiple situations where domestic violence has been the cause of many breakups, broken relationships, and devastated families of all sorts and kinds. I have regrettably stood by and watched children be ripped from the arms of their parents, best friends' lives destroyed, husband and wife crash land into divorce court. It seems like a never-ending cycle. For my own sanity's sake, I've done my own research regarding this devastating life-changing issue. I have come up with a conclusion that would best fit this issue and still preserve the dignity of both parties.

I have over my lifetime, have been both shocked and confused about this subject. Regrettably, I am writing this from a perspective that very few would possibly agree with. However, I feel I need to take this challenge to express how we can best stomp out domestic violence in our homes, communities, and in our country.

Many years ago, before law enforcement became involved in the judge, jury, and Executioner of the domestic parties involved in a domestic violence call, women were marrying and, for the most part, happy and excited to be married, loving their man and of course, their men were doing the same. Though there were cases of domestic violence, most documented cases of domestic violence occurred during a time when alcohol was very prevalent in our communities.

During the time of prohibition, alcohol consumption declined tremendously, and as a result of that, so did the horrific act of domestic violence. There were champions, leaders women who stood strong against domestic violence as well as its hidden culprit, alcohol. However, the story doesn't end there. Alcohol plays a major role in the destruction of families and communities. Nonetheless, I can't truly put the blame on alcohol entirely separate because whatever is in a person is going to come out of that person. In other words, if there is in that person an innate mentality of attacking then, all alcohol does is open the door for the person's true self to be revealed without any inhibitions. Concluding, deep down, this individual's anger, irritation, and frustration are the real culprits that usually aren't seen. As I stated before, a lot of men have self-esteem issues, so speaking with them negatively or what would be perceived as hateful would only promote a more aggressive male. Many women aren't aware of this fact due to that women tend to walk into a very dangerous beehive of male low self-esteem and misguided emotions.

If I can tell my sisters on this planet anything in particular in relation to male low self-esteem and male ego, I would suggest approaching any situation regarding a male with delicate hands. I'm sure a lot of women would say he's not a child; he is a man he should be able to take it if I cursed him out or lose my temper on him. He is a man, he should know never to hit a woman. I would have to agree with that. However, You would also have to remember that he's also a human being, a person with feelings and rarely is his issues regarding himself ever addressed. A great percentage of males find themselves feeling down, feeling left out, hurt, crushed many, many, many times, and then, to add insult to injury, add alcohol to the mix or some other illicit drug, and you have basically a ticking time bomb. The only way you can defuse that time bomb is to use kind words. Ladies, you have to remember that the **Tongue is so powerful**; it can do great things. The tongue has the power to build him up or tear him down. You could choose to build him up with your words; it's your choice.

Caution: if you choose to tear him down, he may retaliate physically. Thus, domestic violence would be result of that.

PUNISH THE ELEPHANT

Chapter 5

Words and actions:

I grew up at a time when People would say that "***sticks and stones may break my bones but words will never harm me!***" That, of course, is a lie. What I found out was that Sticks and stones may break my bones, but words can utterly destroy me.

I

Unlike sticks and stones, words affect the very core of a person. Attacking their self-esteem motivation. Even affecting their will to live. Words have power, great power. Your words have the power to build someone up to believe they could conquer the world, or your words can tear them down making them believe they are nothing and have no reason for living. **WORDS ARE CAPSULES OF INFORMATION AND PIECES OF PICTURES.** Words are extremely important in our relationships. Whether we are talking to the mailman or our spouse, each word has a meaning and each word should be thought about before releasing it into the world. All our relationships depend on it!

There are three kinds of relationships:

Associations:

Friendships:

Long term relationships

For greater clarity, here are their meanings,

Associations: General conversation (weather, sports, shopping, etc..)

Friendships: someone who knows more about you than the general things. Things that are more specific, like your birthday, last name, favorite color or food, and so on...

Long-term relationships: These people know everything about you, even the dirty details. This is the person/people you would commit being open to because they accept you for who you are.

Transparency and or intimacy:

The measuring stick or ruler to determine whether you are in an association, friendship, or long-term relationship is transparency or intimacy.

How transparent you can be with a person determining where you are with them. It determines whether they are associations, friendships, or long-term relationships. How much about the true you that can you divulge? How much you can communicate about your true self with a person determines the level of relationship you are in with that person.

Transparency and or Intimacy is established through communication.

Note:

There's three types of people in this world in regards to communication. There's a reactionary base person, there's a responsive person, there is also a shut down person.

Communication is to a relationship, like blood is to the body.

The human body needs blood to live. Without blood, we would cease to exist. The same goes for relationships. Communication is the blood of a relationship, you must have communication for a relationship to live and to thrive. Just like without blood, you would die. In a relationship, without communication, your relationship would die.

There is absolutely nothing more dangerous to a relationship than lack of communication as well as lack of transparency. Neglecting to communicate causes the relationship to wither and die. Neglecting to be transparent while in a relationship causes your relationship to become stagnant, thus losing its ability to live and grow long-term.

Now, there are two ways and two forms of communication. Writing is part of the non-verbal form. (Remember, we are keeping this simple)!

The two forms of communicating are verbal and non-verbal.

The two ways are negative and positive.

A relationship is like a plant. If you water (positive communication) that plant with fresh water and give it plenty of sunshine (transparency or intimacy), it will thrive and grow.

However, if you pour oil (negative communication) on that plant instead of water, you reduce its sunshine (not transparent or intimate) it will wither and die.

Are you starting to catch on? I cannot very well share with you information regarding family if I cannot assist you in seeing where the problems are in your relationship which causes the family to break up in the first place. **Prevention is better than cure.** We first have to be able to outline what the issues are in our relationship so that we are able to continue to have a prosperous family, and while doing so, we can put all the pieces together to ensure everything runs according to the way that it was intended.

Conclusion: The Weight of Words in Relationships

In this chapter, we discuss the profound impact that words and communication have on our relationships. The age-old adage that "sticks and stones may break my bones, but words will never harm me" proves to be a fallacy; words hold immense power, capable of both uplifting and devastating those we care about. Every interaction—whether casual or intimate—demands our thoughtfulness, as the way we communicate can define the nature and depth of our relationships.

We categorize our connections into associations, friendships, and long-term relationships, with transparency and intimacy serving as vital measures of their strength. The ability to share our true selves with others dictates the level of our bond. Just as blood sustains the body, communication sustains relationships; without it, they stagnate and ultimately wither away.

Our words can either nurture our relationships or poison them. Positive communication, akin to watering a plant with fresh water and providing it sunlight, fosters growth and intimacy. Conversely, negative communication acts like oil, stifling growth and leading to deterioration.

As we navigate our connections, let us remember that effective communication is not merely about speaking; it's about being present, transparent, and genuinely invested in one another. By embracing this understanding, we can prevent misunderstandings and cultivate stronger, more resilient relationships. In a world where words are often taken for granted, let's choose to wield our words with care and intention, ensuring that they uplift rather than harm and foster connections that thrive.

PUNISH THE ELEPHANT

Chapter 6

CONFLICT AND CONFLICT RESOLUTION

A lack of detail expectations

Don't throw the baby out with the bathwater!

There are far too many times I have been involved in relationships with people. While in the relationship (dating), instead of us communicating with each other, we unfortunately immediately walk away, or just rudely hang up the phone, or, in some disconnecting way, we became distant.

If you are in a relationship, the absolute very last thing you want to do in that relationship is to disconnect. You want to at all times keep the lines open. You want to ensure that you are being more than fair to the person you are in a relationship with. Communication is to a relationship, like blood is to the body.

All growing and evolving relationships require patience. I'm sorry to tell you this, there is no way around it. If you genuinely intend to be around the long haul, you're going to have to endure. **You are going to have to make up your mind to be in it all the way 1000 percent, no excuses!** You are also going to need to have detailed expectations.

We, as people, come from different backgrounds, different lifestyles, and different ways of thought. We have different parental upbringings. The differences are always right in the individual eyes of both parties. What I have found to be helpful is if you're going to bring up your personal/traditional, or individual differences. I've found that having a substantial written reference point, such as the Bible if you're a Christian, the Quran if you're a Muslim, and so on, will help! If the beliefs are different try to settle on an agreement between the two. If all else fails, sit down separately and write all the good things regarding your point of view. Combine those positive points. I hope that will help.

To those who walk away, hang up the phone, or just become distant...

How do you expect your relationship to grow when the first sign of trouble you tuck tail and run, hang up the phone or become distant? We all are products of our environment. Taking a moment to pier deeper into what could have started the problem in the first place, screams to your partner that you're on board for the long term with them. Making a stand to communicate in the midst of frustration says to your partner, "I'm not going anywhere"!

I have read somewhere that Heroes do the things that need to be done no matter the consequences.

Challenge yourself to pier deeper into this understanding. We say that we are in a relationship with someone. Yet the word "relationship" has a root word, "relate." The word relate means to understand. When you relate with someone, you understand from their perspective or point of view, what they are attempting to relate to you. For far too long, we have allowed selfishness and lack of self-control to be the norm in our society.

However, if you were to look deeper into your relationship and practice self-control, there isn't any situation you could not overcome. Not even cheating.

Some people have addressed the issue of cheating to me as if it is something new that has never been done. Let's be realistic. Men and women cheat on their prospective partners and have been cheating for years when they feel they are not getting what they need at home.

If you are fantasizing that you are doing what you're supposed to do. But your partner doesn't seem interested or seems to be somewhere else. Chances are you are not doing what you are supposed to be doing with your partner. **Does your partner know your expectations? Do you know your partner's expectations?** We, as so-called independent individuals, have a problem listening to each other. That's the reason why communication is the number one thing in a relationship. so that we can begin to understand the importance of listening to each other. I use the word "listening" because you could hear someone and charge it off as listening, but it's not! Honest listening requires the heart, empathy, placing yourself in that person's situation selflessly, and imagining what it feels like to be them. Being a fellow human being to a fellow human being. Too many times, we have allowed the things that happen in our lives to distract us, such as our job, family issues, paying the mortgage, and many various other things, have a tendency to sway our limited attention. In truth, we shouldn't get so caught up. We all have been placed on this planet to help each other. That's why listening is so very important. By listening, you may have the answer to your partner's problem, and the entire time, you would not have known it. It was said to me once that you have two ears and one mouth; you are to listen twice as much as you speak. Let's try listening, and you will be surprised by what you hear.

I can remember many, many years ago when I was a child. I recalled responding to my parent's disagreement the exact same way I was responding to my girlfriend's disagreement. I didn't see the difference until I sat down one day and thought about the multiple relationships that I had lost frivolously. Each time, I chose to walk away instead of working it out. I was such a coward. I wish I knew back then how childish and immature my simple mind was. There were several things that brought me to the conclusion that the majority of the problems that existed in my relationship came from my inability to work it out. For instance, I have had at least twenty girlfriends in my lifetime. Many people get involved in relationships and, at the most, have three or possibly four if they function well. With me, that wasn't the case. I did not recognize the extreme dysfunction that was in my life and caused me to make the improper choices I was making and yet blame other women because of the decisions that I was making. In other words it was everyone else's fault but mine. When it struck me that it could possibly be my fault, it came through someone who shared with me things regarding relationships. They asked me how long ago was it since I was in high school. I told him it was more than 20 years ago. Then, I was asked, how many relationships have I been in since the high school relationship? Of course, they asked me to name the various relationships and be sure to put my name in with the person I had a relationship with. Once I began to name the first five relationships with my name included with each of them as instructed, it was brought to my attention what each of those relationships and I have in common. Of Course, each of the relationships had one thing in common: me! Then it was brought to my attention where did I think the problem existed.

You see, with that simple exercise, you're able to recognize something simple even if you have had quite a few relationships, such as I have, you can see that possibly the problem could be you.

Which brings me back to the point: how do you resolve conflict? **Conflict resolving is the very essence of a relationship; it is the determiner of whether or not your relationship will make it through the difficult times. Conflict resolution and honest, realistic expectations make it possible to go long-term. Chances are very high that the two individual have not outlined their expectations for each other. Many times, when there's extreme conflict, those individuals who are involved in a relationship have not taken the time to express their expectations to each other. Resolving conflict is a lot easier when you have** *reference points of expectation*s **that were brought to the table at the beginning of the relationship. Attempting to share expectations midway through the relationship could very well keep the problems that you're suffering alive for a while. It is much better to discuss what your expectations are in detail with your partner, write it down, and give it to them. Yes, give them a copy!** I find it equally helpful to write it down and post it somewhere in the home. Somewhere, it could be seen regularly for at least the first year. By having those expectations posted in your house, you say to your partner- "I want this to work"! Not to mention, you give your relationship a true fighting chance to last long term. Many times, good relationships have suffered the tragedy of breakups due to the fact of lack of understanding of the expectations of the other partner. This is a very serious exercise. If you intend on having a fighting chance of making this relationship work please take each bit of information and apply it. Besides, it's not like the way you were doing it was working so wonderful, right?

PUNISH THE ELEPHANT

Chapter 7

Authority in your relationships

I would like to make something plain to those who don't know this. This is also an important piece of the relationship puzzle. It also can make or break a good relationship,

Authority

You can't have Authority without responsibility and accountability.

I have stood back and watched women talk to men. I have repeatedly seen women attempt to fight and fought men. A couple of years ago, I was with a friend, and we went out to have breakfast together. My female friend sat quietly in the restaurant as I was sharing with her the difficulty of the things that transpired the day before. As I was speaking with my female friend calmly in this restaurant, our waitress came up and began to express her frustration concerning her man. Hearing her speak, we stopped talking and looked at each other, amazed. I looked up at our waitress. Smilingly, I said to the waitress, "I'm sure your relationship will work itself out!" Her statement to me was, "It better because when I get home, I'm going to beat him up!" I remember saying to myself, "What did she just say?" So I asked her. I said, "Miss, did you just say you're going to beat your man up?" She's standing in front of me, and my quiet lady friend continued to rant 'about her man. So, I fired off the first torpedo of truth to target that misunderstanding. I asked her, "When did women get so bold?" Then I said before she had the opportunity to answer, "Never mind. I know when they got so bold when they could call the police once they start a fight with the man, and the man will go to jail." Then I turned to my friend who came to breakfast with me and said to her, "Do you know what a person is called in the man's world that starts a fight and talks crazy, threatening a person, then run and call someone to help back them up after they have started that dramatic fight. In a man's world, that person is called a coward. To make it plain, you would be considered weak, lesser than a real man. A punk a** b****, a loser."

In today's society, people believe that having a sense of power in many ways empowers you. However power is something that is given by someone more powerful than you. When one has power and or authority that person is given or delegated that power and or authority due to the character to which they have exhibited, that character is one that could handle having power over another person.

Real Authority submits to authority. False Authority doesn't submit to Real Authority. False Authority can only pretend to submit to Real Authority. False Authority has no reference point for its perverted pretended authority. False Authority cannot be substantiated through any real outside source. Only Real Authority can be substantiated by an outside source separate from itself. When a person has Real or what we call genuine authority, that person's authority can be removed by the individual, individuals, or groups that gave them that authority. Authority is conditional to the person based on their ability to fulfill that authority.

When genuine authority is abused, the individual, individuals, or groups that gave the Authority remove the authoritative person's authority due to the abuse of it. Authority is necessary to sustain and or maintain order. Whether that order is in your house or that order is in the White House. Authority is essential to the order of things. Without genuine authority, our house, community, cities, state, and country will unravel. *Authorities main position is to continue to maintain the order that has been established.*

This part is the most exciting for me. This is the part that is very powerful, it seemingly by itself changes everything. Once you understand the importance of order, you will be able to see before your very eyes the coming together of your family, your relationships, your friendships, and your partnership. This is the single most iconic thing in the entire book. To miss this part is to miss it all. The reason why I am so very excited about this part of the book is because most of the problems happening in our relationships are due to the fact that we don't know when to do what. We just tend to believe that we have an established role that has no genuine basis. An established role that gives us the perceived (False) authority. Once you realize that authority is something that someone else has to give you, then you're able to reflect upon the multiple times that you could have exhibited some form of (false) authority that was not delegated/given to you. Usually, when one does exhibit (False Authority), it causes reason for conflict. (Because it's not real Authority) We know very well that conflict leads to arguments, arguments lead to fights, fights lead ultimately to destruction of your relationship.

Side note: To all the wonderful ladies, this is a side note. MEN LOVE PEACE….

PUNISH THE ELEPHANT

Chapter 8:

THREE FORMS OF AUTHORITY

God's, Man's, and Woman's.

I have included a diagram to help you see what I mean.

In exploring the dynamics of Authority within the family structure, it is essential to recognize the three distinct levels: **God's Authority, Man's Authority, and Woman's Authority.**

Each plays a critical role in shaping the family structure and environment and ensuring its stability and growth.

At the top of the hierarchy is **God's Authority**, which serves as the ultimate guiding force. This Authority transcends all other authorities, establishing a framework for how individuals should conduct themselves. Within this divine order, we find the roles of **A Lady** and **A Gentleman**.

A **Lady** embodies grace and respect, not only for herself but also for the men in her life. She understands the importance of her carefully chosen words and actions, using them to uplift and nurture rather than to harm. Her demeanor reflects a deep reverence for God's design, allowing her to foster a space where both genders can thrive. This respect is not merely given; it is earned through her consistent comforting behavior and the way she engages with the world around her.

Conversely, a **Gentleman** recognizes his position under God's Authority and the responsibilities that accompany it. He understands that true authority lies not only in physical power but also in the ability to show compassion and humility. A gentleman takes his role seriously, guiding those under his authority with wisdom and integrity. His actions reflect his commitment to a higher purpose, ensuring that he approaches both God and his responsibilities with the utmost respect and care.

Moving down the hierarchy, we arrive at **Man's Authority**. This Authority is rooted in the Biblical mandate for men to dominate the earth and lead their families. It encompasses the responsibility of raising children within the framework of divine order. A **Man's Authority** is not about exerting control but rather about guiding his family in a way that aligns with God's principles. This includes instilling discipline and values in children and ensuring they grow up with a strong moral compass.

Finally, we have **Woman's Authority**, which is primarily focused on nurturing and guiding children. A woman's influence in a child's life is profound; her ability to comfort, encourage, and nurture shapes the next generation. While her authority is specific to her relationship with her children, it is essential to recognize that it complements the authority of man and God. A mother's nurturing presence creates an environment where children can flourish and develop their own understanding of respect and authority.

In summary, these three forms of Authority—***God's, Man's, and Woman's***—create a balanced family structure. Each has its role and significance, contributing to the overall health and harmony of the family unit. Understanding and respecting these dynamics is crucial for fostering a loving and supportive environment where every member can thrive.

MALE		FEMALE
•———————	GOD'S AUTHORITY	———————•
GENTLEMAN		LADY

•———————	MAN'S AUTHORITY	———————•
MAN		WOMEN

•———————	WOMEN'S AUTHORITY	———————•
BOY		GIRL

PUNISH THE ELEPHANT

Chapter 9

Independent or interdependent?

What ever happened to the days when people would celebrate the coming of age? When people would celebrate the real meaning of becoming a man or woman?

Feminism:The true definition of Feminism is a celebration of womanhood. It is the coming of age. A right to passage.

Masculism:The coming of age for a male, right to passage, manhood.

Perverted masculism :

A distorted view of masculism. Perverse perspective of what a Male is. Someone who isn't a Male acts in accordance with the perceived rules of a male by way of word and sometimes action.

Social independence

That seems insane. Those contradictions of words. Think about those two words for a moment. Social and Independence. Social is the congregation of people. Independence is the absence of those people. Go figure...

There are just too many lies to pick apart these days. If you don't believe me. You have only to look at any hamburger commercial. You know as well as I do that what is advertised in the commercials don't come close to what you really get. Yet, people are lining up to receive the next lie that's interwoven with the last. *No one in conventional society is independent.* If we are anything, we are interdependent. To claim one to be independent in the United States of America, you would have to live like The Amish. Even they aren't independent. Just in case you haven't noticed lately, due to their multiple commercials. The Amish are selling heaters therefore, they now seemingly depend on the rest of the country. If not the world, for monetary reasons, so they may continue to live their supposedly independent lifestyle.

For the rest of us, get real! You are so far from independent. **The word independent means "free-standing"**. It literally means that in no way, shape, form, or fashion do you need anything outside of yourself to exist. That would translate, you need no grocery stores, you need no gas station, you need no furniture store, no electrical company, nothing but just you yourself. It's like building your own home. Growing your own food. Building your own shoes or drawing your daily water from a well. We live in a society where a portion of the women can't even cook, let alone go to a well to draw water. I guess it's much easier to live that lie than to swallow the truth.

Considering that's not the reality in the United States of America the facts are you are very interdependent. Now, if you are interdependent, that means that you rely on more than just one entity. You rely on everyone. I really hate to say it this way. Some literally and others figuratively point being that you rely on everyone. That's what interdependence means. So I'm sure you believe that you are independent until you actually get the real definition of independent, which hasn't been tinkered with by those that today support your brainwashing in the now new feminist, male hating, yet male imitating movement.

Please don't misunderstand me. I have great respect in regards to the women of old as well as the women today. I believe in the movement for women to receive equal pay for equal work.

I'm not against that at all. Nor am I against women being treated equal in any setting. I believe in being fair across the board. That's why I believe that we all should be fair and equal to each other. We need to equally coexist. The feminist movement was the type of movement that promoted equality. It was the type of movement in which women wanted their fair wages for a hard day's work. They were not asking for handout or special consideration. They just wanted to be treated fairly. Not a piece of meat. Or overlook because they were women or girls. The type of movement that was inspirational, hard-fought, sincere as well as long overdue. How can I ever be against that?

Today so-called feminists have become everything except for the high character and moral women were during that time. There is only a spark where the flame was. Today's women have forgotten what it was like to be a woman originally in the first place. Meaning, unfortunately have adopted an ideology that don't fit them. This ideology I have nicely and unapologetically coined as perverted masculism.

In this book, in the chapter, "**Authority in Your Relationship**," I make an attempt to express what authority really is. Many women have noticed the Authority that males have or other women have and have wanted to claim it for themselves. However, it's just a little more difficult than that. You see, the feminist movement don't teach women that along with the authority that they are exhibiting, there also is accountability and responsibility. Today's feminists won't learn that from the media or any other entity that would enlighten them to truly be the women that they were called to be. Women of strength and knowledge. A caliber of women that says, I uphold the mantle of my fore mothers in womanhood, and I launch off of this mantle into the future, improving the lifestyles of other women. I do this in honor of our fore mothers, not as a distorted view of a man, perverted masculism, but as a woman, not using anything that men use as a form of glory. Reaching within self and bringing forth a true woman. A woman that embraces who she is. One that's not identified by how masculine she can act. A woman that's comfortable being a woman. It's time to sweep the perversion out the door of your relationships. Let's try a fresh approach. Let's try to make a stand for the old values that have worked for over hundreds of thousands of years. Why not give it a shot? It's not like this new way is working today, anyway.

Don't believe me, look around. I will even make it easier than that for you. Do the math: 79 % of marriages crash land into divorce court within the first five years these days. Yes 79%. Before the 60s in this country, there were very few divorces, less than 10%. Mainly because you had to prove infidelity on the other partner to get a divorce. Or some evil crime against you to get out of a marriage. So people treated it more like the institution that it really is, and not like the, "You don't give me what I want, I'm out of here!" or if you don't praise me and spoil me no matter how unwifely I act, game it is now! You had to stick it out! That's how they made it 50 years.

What happened to us?

When Ronald Reagan was Governor of California, he signed a bill that said it was ok to divorce for any reason, which he later regretted. But too late. The damage was done. The no-fault bill gave women any excuse to leave a marriage as opposed to sticking it out, working it out idea. Before that bill, if she felt unhappy for whatever reason, she could file or petition to get a divorce. Of course, as usual, other states followed suit, as they still do today. This just so happened to be very convenient as the use of hallucinating drugs (tapping into your inner self) in the country was increasing, as well as the push to find oneself (selfishness) was becoming ever-popular. Along with the free love movement, translation: free sex. Now you have a recipe for divorce. The stats show the rise after the 60s. Shortly after the rise of divorce, women began having children out of wedlock. The single-parent era was born and is now on the rise. It is still rising to this very day. Selfishness will always cause destruction whenever it has its way. No matter if it is in a relationship, society, or a business. The price is always too high.

We are all loving and caring humans. We can make this work if we really want to.

Men are the gatekeepers of the household.

Remove the male father/husband (teacher of discipline and self-control), and you get the social problem we have today. I don't feel a need to mention gangs, high prison rates, underdeveloped males and females, childhood obesity, reckless relationships, domestic violence, early youth prostitution, a deteriorating community, a deteriorating economy, and world status. You see, countries are made up of states. States are made up of cities. And cities are made up of communities. Communities are made up of families. It's that simple. Look at the state of the families, and you can see where the country is going. It's not difficult to understand if you're willing to look. We need to get back to family. It's the only thing that will save us all. Family is selfless, not selfish. It is the one thing on this planet that you can be involved in and change the lives of all those involved.

You only get one life, one opportunity to make a difference.

The company doesn't care if you live or die. Nonetheless, those you leave every day to make money would love just to be with you more than any dollar you can produce. While falling for the media's lies, you are supposedly making their lives better by not being in it. Mostly, life is better when you are in it. Not away making someone else rich, who's probably home with their family, enjoying the wealth that you're sacrificing your family to provide them. Can you see how you may have been cheated?

Furthermore, let us revisit the essence of what it means to be truly independent versus interdependent. Independence, in its purest form, is a myth in our interconnected world. It is a fleeting concept that many cling to as a badge of honor, yet the reality is that our lives are woven together in a complex tapestry of relationships and dependencies. We are not solitary beings; we are part of a larger community, a family, a society that thrives on collective strength.

Feminism, at its heart, should celebrate the richness of womanhood, fostering empowerment while embracing the invaluable qualities that define women. It is not about forsaking femininity or adopting a distorted version of masculinity. True feminism honors

the past, recognizing the struggles and triumphs of those who paved the way for women. It is about lifting each other up, nurturing the innate wisdom and strength that resides within every woman, and refusing to conform to ideologies that obscure women's identities.

As we reflect on the state of our relationships, we must understand that authority comes with accountability. The pursuit of equality should not result in a battle of the sexes but rather an alliance that encourages mutual respect and understanding. We must strive for a balance where both men and women can peacefully coexist harmoniously, honoring their roles without succumbing to societal pressures that dictate otherwise.

The statistics tell a sobering story: the rise of divorce, single-parent homes, and disintegrating family structures. These are not merely numbers; they represent lives affected by the choices we make—or fail to make. It's time to challenge the narrative that has led us astray. We must embrace a return to the values that once fortified our families and communities, promoting selflessness over selfishness.

In a world that often prioritizes individual gain over collective well-being, let us remember the importance of being present for those we love. True fulfillment comes not from accolades or material success but from the connections we nurture and the love we share. The legacy we leave behind is not measured in wealth or status but in the lives we touch and the bonds we forge.

So, I invite you to reflect: What kind of woman—or man—do you aspire to be? Are you ready to embrace your identity fully and authentically, not defined by societal expectations but by your own values? If we seek to reclaim our relationships and our lives, we must first understand the importance of community, family, and the strength of being interdependent. Let us celebrate our differences, uplift one another, and build a future where both women and men can thrive together.

In unity lies our power, and in recognition of our shared humanity, we can create a world that honors the true spirit of feminism—one that is rooted in love, respect, and a commitment to nurturing the very fabric of our society.

PUNISH THE ELEPHANT

Chapter 10

For the men.......

Many years ago, when I was with my best friend. I learned some very important things about the dynamics of relationships between men and women.

In another portion of this book, I speak directly to women. Now, I'm having to be equal and speak directly to the men.

Men, How will you be able to help your woman, make her happy, and respect her entirely without inside information? This inside information will help you greatly. For many, it will help you not to be violent. For others, it would explain something that went bad or wrong in past relationships that could very well be salvageable.

There are so many dynamic situations that this information could empower you as a man. I'm hoping you will truly process what I'm saying.

We, as men, are 85% logic, 15% emotions. As a male, when you fall in love, care deeply for, or are extremely infatuated with someone, we are only 15% emotional. If there is a problem/situation/serious trouble in our relationships, we are totally thrown off. As men, most of us have experienced, to some degree, the brokenness we feel when that person who we have allowed to get close to us betrays us with their words, actions, or inaction.

It's a feeling of hopelessness, desperation, and despair that crippled our ability to see past the emotional walls that have surprisingly sprung up, ensnared and captured us completely.

At times, we would logically process that this person is making our lives extremely difficult. Yet, how to deal with this is the question.

I'm sure you remember the interview in 1988 with Robin Givens and Mike Tyson on 60 mins. The interviewer was Barbara Walters. While interviewing the couple on live television, Miss Givens was talking about Mike Tyson and how he was just a horrible person. On live television, yes, live television. She sat comfortably next to him as he stared into the camera quietly, no doubt in love, in front of the television audience around the world. She said many difficult things right to his face. He seemed love-struck. Completely paralyzed by love, which is attributed to 15% emotion that was at work in his life. It's the reason why we believe some relationships make you weak. You know what I mean.

We, as men and women, process things differently. As stated earlier, the title reflects we are males, and because we are males, we process things through logic. In past times, I've used examples. Examples such as, you decide to take your woman to the mall. While at the mall, both of you are window shopping. Your woman looks up and sees a bridal shop. Her thoughts are on how beautiful those dresses look. "How lovely," she would look in one or more of those dresses or, possibly, how wonderful her bridesmaid would look in other dresses throughout the store. While being her partner, your thoughts immediately turn to how much this might cost me. As logical creatures we are consistently confronted by The reality of numbers and or expenses. What would be the cost of something or assessing the situation from a logical perspective. In an attempt to be the very best in everything we do, we attempt to try to find the best possible outcome. An outcome that will benefit us as men as well as our relationship communities and our families. Mostly looking at all our situations from the perspective of logic.

As a man, you realize and recognize that knowing this information could assist you in making decisions relating to your relationship. As not to be taken by surprise emotionally as we males generally are. One of the most positive things that has happened in my life was having a friend of mine, whom I care for and love greatly, sit down and talk to me regarding how women think. She shared with me some very fundamental things that I hadn't even recognize until after she mentioned them. One of the things that she shared with me was how women process information. I can recall several times she mentioned to me about how she felt trapped inside her own body. As strange as that may sound, I gave it some serious thought. What she was attempting to say to me is, inside of her is, an idea of what she wants to do. However, her emotions would take hold of her, forcing her to move without thinking. Literally, her emotions would move her in a direction without her having the ability at that moment to process thoroughly what she is doing or saying. As she was expressing that to me, I looked at her strangely because I had not until that moment understood entirely what she was attempting to share.

Later, after processing thoroughly what she was expressing to me, I recognized what she was generally saying. What she was saying is that her emotions have a greater ability to move her without her logic. In other words, what she was saying was she is an emotional creature and being an emotional creature has a disadvantage sometimes in relationships. She's not completely able to move according to the way that we males may move. Once I understood where she was coming from, then I could completely understand why she would say something that I believed would be out of sorts or do something that I believed was unnecessary. I was forced to recognize that she didn't do it on purpose. It was a reaction in her room of emotions. Her emotions made her do it! Against her will at times. So, I was forced to give her grace instead of war.

All emotions are valid. Imagine driving a bus. All your emotions are on that bus. Happiness, sadness, irritation, anger, lust, selfishness, compassion, etc…

As a man you should always be driving the bus. You have to always remember who's driving the bus. Is anger driving the bus? Is lust driving or selfishness behind the wheel? Is compassion driving the bus? Who is driving the bus in your life? Is it you or your emotions????

With women, it's different. With women, most times, their emotions are driving the bus. Sometimes, anger, irritation, or frustration is driving the bus. Sometimes compassion and deep affection are driving the bus. However, sometimes selfishness has completely taken over the wheel. It's different with women. Their life journey is different. 85% of the time, an emotion is behind the wheel. 85% of the time, their logic is not in the driver's seat. Now, do you understand?

In this chapter, we discuss the complexities of male-female dynamics, emphasizing the importance of understanding emotional versus logical processing in relationships. The narrative highlights that we, as men, are predominantly logical beings who often struggle to navigate the emotional landscapes of our partners. This disconnect can lead to misunderstandings and conflicts, particularly when we men are faced with emotionally charged situations that challenge our logical nature.

I have personal reflections and experiences illustrating how awareness of these differences can empower men to approach relationships with greater empathy and understanding. By recognizing that women often process emotions more intensely, we men can learn to respond with grace rather than conflict, fostering healthier interactions.

In conclusion, the essence of this chapter resonates with a call to action for men: "Drive the bus of your emotions." Take control of your emotional responses and be aware of who or what is influencing your decisions in relationships. By doing so, you can create a supportive environment for both yourself and your partner, ultimately leading to a more fulfilling and harmonious connection. The message is clear: understanding and communication are key to bridging the emotional divide, allowing love and respect to finally flourish.

PUNISH THE ELEPHANT

CHAPTER 11

Professional business woman/A wife (soft girl) needed

Hoping to discuss the difference and why it's important to know the difference.

You see, one focuses on the job, money, environment at the job, fulfilling quota, and pleasing her supervisor. Dressing to always look professional, acting in a business like manner. Dogs eat dogs mentally to survive the business world.

The other does the opposite.

Instead of pleasing her supervisor, she seeks to please her husband. Instead of focusing on her environment at work, she focuses on her environment at home. Instead of filling a quota, she's filling her refrigerator, her husband's stomach, and wifely obligations.

Instead of dressing to always look professional, she dresses to get and keep his attention.

Instead of acting in a business manner, she acts in a (soft girl) wifely manner.

In the modern world, the roles of a businesswoman and a wife can often seem to exist in stark contrast, each embodying unique strengths and challenges. Understanding these differences is not only essential for navigating personal and professional relationships but also for appreciating the distinct energies each role brings to the table.

The Businesswoman: Assertive and Aggressive

In the realm of business, the professional woman is a force to be reckoned with. She thrives in a competitive environment, driven by ambition and the need to succeed. Her daily life revolves around meeting quotas, fulfilling job responsibilities, and climbing the corporate ladder. She dresses meticulously to project professionalism, opting for tailored suits and polished shoes that exude authority and competence.

Her mindset is one of resilience; it's a dog-eat-dog world where she must assert herself to survive. The boardroom is her battleground, and her language is one of negotiation and strategy. She focuses on pleasing her supervisors, anticipating their needs, and delivering results that will elevate her career. Every decision she makes is calculated, aimed at maximizing her potential and securing her place in a competitive landscape.

The Wife: Laid-Back and Nurturing (Soft girl)

In contrast, the wife embodies a different energy—one that is nurturing, supportive, and deeply connected to her family. Rather than striving for corporate accolades, her focus shifts to her home and the emotional well-being of her loved ones. She seeks to please her husband, creating an environment where love, warmth, and comfort flourish.

Her approach to life is not about fulfilling quotas but rather about filling her refrigerator and ensuring her husband's needs are met—emotionally and physically. The attire she chooses is often softer, reflecting her femininity and inviting intimacy. Rather than a suit, she may opt for a dress that highlights her curves, drawing her partner's attention and affection.

While the businesswoman operates in a world defined by metrics and power dynamics, the wife embodies a more organic, flowing manner of being. She prioritizes connection over competition, focusing on nurturing relationships rather than climbing a corporate ladder. Her actions are guided by love, empathy, and a desire to create a harmonious home.

The Importance of Recognizing the Difference

Acknowledging the distinction between these two roles is vital. Each woman, whether in the boardroom or the living room, plays a crucial role in her own right. The businesswoman teaches us the value of ambition, resilience, and assertiveness—qualities that are essential in a fast-paced world. Conversely, the wife (soft girl) reminds us of the importance of nurturing, emotional intelligence, and the power of feminine energy.

In conclusion, recognizing the differences between a businesswoman and a wife is crucial for personal growth and understanding. Each role offers unique insights into the strengths and values that women bring to both their professional and personal lives. By celebrating and balancing these aspects, women can truly become the best versions of themselves—encouraging, nurturing, and empowered. Being a massive, unflinching asset to the structured family.

PUNISH THE ELEPHANT

Chapter 12:

The Ring, the Paper, and the Vow

Let's get married... wait, not yet!"

Long term vs short term relationships

When we think of marriage, we often envision the ring, the paper, and the vow. Yet, what truly sustains a long-lasting relationship goes beyond these symbols. The reality is that without a solid foundation, all the rings and vows in the world can't guarantee a successful marriage.

The Foundation of Long-Term Relationships

Before we even think about the ring, the paper and the vow it's essential to build a strong foundation for a long-term relationship. Communication, realistic expectations, and patience are not just buzzwords; they are the cornerstones of lasting love.

Many of us dream of finding our soulmate and envision a life together filled with love and joy. But too often, we dive headfirst into relationships without truly understanding who we are committing to. We may have grand ideas about love, but neglecting to know each other authentically can lead to heartache.

Throughout history, marriage has evolved. Some couples were brought together for family alliances, while others chose partners based on love and compatibility. Regardless of the circumstances, many marriages have endured long after the initial excitement faded. In the past, divorce was stigmatized, and couples worked hard to maintain their unions, often for the sake of their children and family honor.

Understanding the Male Perspective on Marriage

To grasp the complexities of relationships, we must consider how men perceive marriage. It's a common sentiment among men that marriage is a significant commitment. A phrase that often embodies this perspective is: "Why buy the cow when you can get the milk for free?"

This saying reflects a mindset that highlights the perceived risks and responsibilities of commitment. For many men, the idea of marriage involves not just the emotional connection but also the need to provide security and stability for their families.

When a man says, "I do," it signifies a deep commitment. He is declaring that no one else comes before you, and he is ready to protect and support you. Men who take this vow seriously are aligning their lives with the promise they make at the altar.

Short-Term vs. Long-Term Relationships: A Vehicle Analogy

To illustrate the difference between short-term and long-term relationships, let's consider a vehicle. Renting a car is different from owning one. When you rent, you generally return it in the same condition, only enjoying the ride without making significant alterations.

In relationships, some individuals behave like rented cars. They are not invested in making changes or growing together. If a partner is not challenging you or helping you grow, it may signal a short-term mindset.

In contrast, a committed partner is like a car you own. Together, you invest in each other, making modifications to ensure long-term comfort and compatibility. This process of change requires willingness and openness from both sides.

The Importance of Trust and Compatibility

For men, the desire for a long-term relationship is often tied to trust. They seek partners who are not easily swayed by external influences and who are committed to building a life together. Many men have learned to be cautious in relationships, preferring partners who respect their need for autonomy while also fostering a supportive environment.

It's essential to recognize that strength in a partner doesn't equate to dominance or control. True strength lies in mutual respect and the ability to communicate effectively.

In conclusion, the journey toward a fulfilling long-term relationship requires effort from both partners. Understanding each other's perspectives, building a solid foundation, and being willing to grow together are vital steps toward a lasting union. Remember, the commitment symbolized by the ring and the vow is just the beginning; it's the work you put in afterward that truly defines your relationship.

PUNISH THE ELEPHANT

Chapter 13

The Four Roles of Family

Let us first start this understanding by discussing what a family is. Family is a father's unit or community. The "Fa" in family means father. The "mily" means community or unit. Therefore, the word Family means Father's unit or community.

There are only four roles in a family. The first role is a father. **The father's role is very important because his job is to *CREATE*, *ESTABLISH*, and *MAINTAIN* the safety and security of his household.** To better understand the father's role, we must first get a definition of what a father means. **The word father means Source, originator, and sustainer.** I like to refer to him as **S.O.S.**

We all know that an **S.O.S.** is used whenever there is an emergency. Whenever conventional ways of communication have been lost, and an emergency is needed to summon for help then an **S. O. S.** is used. A family has an **S.O.S.** system as well. That **S.O.S.** system is the father. Let me give you an example: when a child is in trouble, the child cries out for their mother. However, when the mother or wife is in trouble, she screams for her husband. Now, when the husband is in trouble, he calls on GOD. Again, the child cries out and says, **"MAMMA"**! When the wife/mother is in trouble, she cries out and says, **"HONEY"**! But when the husband/father is in trouble, he cries out, **"OH GOD"**! I'm sure that you can see the order here.

Order is extremely important in any situation, from the beginning of life until death and beyond. So it is with the family. There is order in the family. **REMEMBER, ANYTHING THAT'S NOT IN ORDER IS OUT OF ORDER.** However, in today's society very little order has been established due to the misconceptions of what the definition of family really means.

The most important thing to remember about the father's household is that you cannot have a family without a father. The reason is because the definition of family means father's unit or community and it takes a living seed to produce a living child. Without a living seed, you cannot produce a living child. Let's take a moment and look at what a father is. If you can remember earlier, we discussed the definition of a father. The father's definition is **source, originator, and sustainer.** He is the source of the living child; he is the originator of the living child, and it is his job to sustain that living child. Once again, he is the,

SOURCE, ORIGINATOR and SUSTAINER. (S.O.S.).

When a man takes the responsibility of becoming a father and husband, the very first thing he does is go before his woman and ask for her hand in marriage. This asking her hand in marriage is the beginning of the family. He, from the time he ask her hand in marriage, requests that she take his last name. Once doing so she is no longer responsible for her own welfare. It is his job to take full responsibility for her and all the offspring that will be birth as a result of his seed.

IT TAKES A LIVING SEED TO PRODUCE A LIVING CHILD.

Once he takes responsibility for her, it's his job to **create, establish, and maintain** her and the future children's safety and security. He is obligated to create an environment where she will be safe. He is also *obligated* to sustain that environment in *safety and security*. However, his obligations don't end there. *He must also create, establish, and maintain her emotional and spiritual security as well as her physical security.* The father/husband's role doesn't just end with his wife. He has to also ensure the safety and security of the children that he has brought forth through his seed.

Along with the understanding that he has to **create, establish, and maintain** the Safety and Security of his household. He has to also be willing to be open to new forms or ways that will help him achieve that goal in an ever-growing society and world. A father's role is the backbone of any family, and without a father, there is no family. It takes a father to have a family.

Now that we have addressed the role of the Father. I would like to discuss with you another role that's equally important. The role of the devoted, compassionate, loving Mother. The Mother's role could be equally impactful and devastating to the child who does not receive the essential love from the luxury of a mother.

At this point, I would like to share with you an example of what I mean by being equal. I believe that the mother's role is equal to the father's role. The reason I believe that is because in life, we have to be balanced. Our days are balanced with night. Good is balanced with bad, and right is balanced with wrong. Happiness is balanced with sadness. There is so much balance in our universe, in our world, and in our lives. A child should also have that balance. A child should have the balance of a father and a mother. Unmistakably, a balanced child will see his or her world from a balanced perspective and be able to assist in helping mankind develop and search through multiple problems that we have in this society. Considering there is a balance, the chances are that child will not develop biasness' for one parent or the other. Thus, that child won't participate in useless rhetoric about one gender or the other. But will be able to focus on problems themselves and not attach a stereotypical, sociological deficient view of one's gender or race.

Getting back to the focus on equality, here's an example of what I wanted to express earlier. Let's take a moment and look at both of our hands. Stretch your hands in front of you and look at them. You will notice that you have a right and left hand. Your right hand is uniquely different from your left hand. Even though your right hand is uniquely different from your left hand, they both are equal. Your left hand and your right hand both have to come together to make sure that you can best do your day-to-day job. There are places on your body that you cannot reach with your left hand, and there are places on your body that you cannot reach with your right hand. However, with both of your hands working, it is possible to reach all parts of your body with your hands and get things done including cleaning your body by the use of both hands. I hope I didn't lose you. Simply put, I have yet to see anyone wash one of their hands without the other hand or in other words, it takes both hands to make sure that both hands are clean. Make no mistake about it; a mother's role is equally important as the father's role, yet uniquely different.

The Mother's role is essential and is defined as NURTURER, ENCOURAGER, and COMFORTER. I like to refer to her role as N.E.C. The mother's role is very complex. The mother's role requires her to always be the motivator, if you will. She can, at times, exhibit the father's role. However, the role that she best fits and knows naturally is her role.

At this time, I would like to bring to your attention a few things that I've discussed in the past in relation to these two roles. In relation to each role, I would like to discuss with you or bring to your attention something that we experience every day. For example, let's discuss the mailman and the firemen. As you are aware, every job or role has its qualifications and job description. Not to mention the uniform that was issued to best perform that role or job. A fireman has to meet certain qualifications before he is able to wear the uniform and put out fires. A mailman has to have certain qualifications before he can wear a uniform and deliver your mail. What would happen if you woke up tomorrow and saw a fireman delivering your mail? Or your house was on fire, and a mailman drove over to put it out.

Surely, at that point, you would have questions. You would wonder why, with the established orders of things in this society, why there is a mailman putting out a fire or a fireman delivering your mail. You would probably say that doesn't make any sense. Now, you cannot accept that illogical switching of roles outside of your house, and yet it is accepted inside your house today. Please don't misunderstand me. It is possible to have the character of the other role to a degree, however, not for a long period of time. Obviously, if the switching of roles continues there would be a breakdown in the balance of how things are. Confusion would automatically set in, and things would be Neglected, Ignored and eventually Discarded simply because the people that are in those roles were not qualified or equipped for those roles. I hope you understand my point.

Some people say, why would you bring up something like that, you are disturbing the order of the way things are now? There was a long time ago, a friend of mine told me something. He said if it's not broken, don't fix it. Well, let's look around. It's pretty obvious that the family structure is broken. It's pretty obvious that in today's society, there are more problems than solutions for the average family. The idea of it is not broken, don't fix it really doesn't apply to the American family today. Unfortunately, the reality is the American family is very broken. The only way that the American family will have the opportunity of being fixed is that some things have to be outlined. One of the things that need to be outlined in the American family is the structure it its roles.

There is order in everything as I stated earlier. There will continue to be order in everything. A fact remains: if we ignore the order, then what we're basically doing is destroying ourselves. I personally have a problem with self-destruction or self-destructive behavior. I feel that if we ought to at any point make a turnaround, we have to begin at the core; the root core of our society is our home is our families. The one problem that we're having the greatest difficulty in turning things around today in our society is the family unit.

Laws are on the books and have been on the books to accommodate the misconception, the destruction, and, unfortunately, the brokenness that permeates our relationships, families, and our communities. We have a responsibility as responsible adults to do whatever it takes while on this planet for this short period of time. To live in such a way as to make sure that our families are number one. That may mean to sacrifice. We may have to sacrifice our friend's views of us. We may have to sacrifice the ideas that have been forced down our throats by the movies, media, internet, magazine, television as well as radio. We may have to sacrifice everything we know as comfort and become uncomfortable for a little while so that we may get our families back on track. I'm not suggesting an easy road in these times. I am stating, if anything, the most difficult road possible.

Coming to terms with the reality that we have fallen off track from our heritage, we have fallen off track from family. From what we were intended to originally say great things about us as a people, it shuts down the notion that we are good people nature by and that because we are good people by nature, all we have to do is go back to our original goodness and go back to ourselves. This, of course, is a lie.

The fact is we are not good by nature. We are bad by Nature. That is the reason why there are so many different religions in the world. The reason why churches, mosques, and synagogues are packed week after week. The reason why there is such a thing as police officers, judges, lawyers. If we were good by nature, no one would be starving, homeless, jobless, rich or poor. If we were good by nature, there would be no such thing as civil rights, Martin Luther King Jr., or any other civil rights leader. If we were good by nature, there would be no such things as murderers, rapists, or any other heinous crimes against each other. There would be no reason for guns or the death penalty in this country or any place in the world. Again, the fact is we are not good by nature, honestly, who are we fooling?

PUNISH THE ELEPHANT

Chapter 14

BRIDGES

The four roles of family continue. The role of the son and daughter is explained

Men/Women build bridges. Boys/girls burn bridges.

In this chapter, I am making an attempt to express the complex dynamics of a family or person affected by the behaviors of an irresponsible son and/or an arrogant daughter. To effectively convey their roles, it's essential to create identifiable markers for you the reader, allowing you to recognize these traits across varying ages.

The Irresponsible Son(Boy)

No matter the age!

1. **Bridge Burner:** This son is characterized by his tendency to burn bridges, signifying a lack of commitment and foresight. You can identify him through actions like abandoning responsibilities, refusing to engage in family discussions, or making impulsive decisions that alienate him from family support.

2. **Defiance and Rebellion**: He displays a rebellious attitude, often challenging authority figures. This can manifest in dismissive comments towards parents or a refusal to follow household rules, regardless of his age.

3. **Discontent and Dissatisfaction**: The son frequently exhibits feelings of discontent and dissatisfaction, whether it's with his current situation, relationships, or family dynamics. He may

vocalize complaints or engage in self-destructive behavior, reflecting an inner turmoil that manifests outwardly.

4. **Lack of Accountability**: He avoids taking responsibility for his actions, often blaming circumstances or others for his failures. This can be highlighted through excuses or shifting blame, making it clear that he is not mature enough to own his own actions.

The Arrogant Daughter(girl)
No matter the age!

1. **Bridge Burner**: Similar to her brother, the daughter also burns bridges, but her approach is more about asserting superiority. She may dismiss family values, prefer peer validation over family support, and cut ties with those she deems beneath her.

2. **Arrogance and Superiority**: The daughter often exhibits an inflated sense of self-worth, leading her to be condescending towards others. She might make derogatory remarks about the family or express disdain for their values, showcasing her rebellious nature.

3. **Defiance and Entitlement**: She challenges family norms and expectations, often demanding special treatment. This entitlement can lead to confrontations with parents, where she justifies her actions with a belief that she deserves more than what is given.

Commonalities in Behavior

Please pay close attention to this:

Both the irresponsible son and the arrogant daughter share some common traits that reflect a lack of maturity and emotional intelligence. They can be characterized by:

Emotional Manipulation: The son/daughter may engage in emotional manipulation to get their way, using guilt or pity to sway you or family members. This behavior can be identified by their ability to create conflict or drama, making themselves appear the victim while deflecting responsibility.

- **Irresponsibility:** Their inability to manage their actions leads to chaos within the family structure.

- **Rebellious Attitude**: Both resist authority, showcasing a desire for independence that turns into defiance.

- **Emotional Turmoil**: They may struggle with internal feelings of inadequacy, leading to destructive behaviors that affect family dynamics.

Both do not keep their word.

Conclusion

By clearly defining the roles of the irresponsible son and the arrogant daughter with these markers, you will be able to identify their behaviors regardless of age. This will help you understand the implications of such actions on family dynamics, allowing for a deeper engagement with the themes presented in this book. Your honest and thorough exploration of these traits serves as a powerful reflection on the challenges families face in navigating the complexities of relationships. I hope this will help.

PUNISH THE ELEPHANT

Chapter 15

THE BOND

What God has joined together, let no man separate!

BOND

join or be joined securely to something else,

synonyms:

Join, fasten, fix, affix, attach, secure, bind, stick, fuse

It's all about "THE BOND"

I can remember when I was a young man. I somehow found myself sick. My illness was so very odd to me. One day, I was feeling good; the next my body was feeling as if I had gained 100lbs at the time that I had fallen sick. It was during those dreaded, dangerously stupid teenage years. I had turned 17 and no longer was living at home. As it turned out, I still knew my mother would worry about me deep down. So, I worked my way back to my parents' house in hopes of some help. Once there, my mother thought I was being stupid like I had been so many times before. She thought I was playing her for a fool. But I wasn't. I had contracted a spinal disease.

Days passed while I stayed at my parent's house. Around the third day, I could barely move my legs. I had to ask my brother to help me to the restroom. Finally, my stepdad protested. And took me to the hospital, where I collapsed.

I awaken in a hospital bed accompanied by a strong convulsion. My God, they were so very painful. I had been in a coma for five days before I awaken. Followed by Three complete days of extremely painful, nonstop torturous convulsing. Each convulsion was equally painful as the last. I finally begged God to help. My mother was in the room as I made my plea, and she began to tell me about where she was worshiping and offered me prayer. I gladly accepted.! God must have heard us because within 24hrs my convulsions subsided until I was able to sit up and enjoy a conversation most of the day.

Finally, I was released from the hospital, and immediately, we went to my mother's church to show my gratitude to her God. While there, I noticed a young man my age and his wife holding hands and showing deep affection. That's when I desired that which they had. They had a bond. I, for the longest time, thought it was just your run of the mill relationship. Deep down, however, I knew it was much greater. I was too young and to naive to relationships to know what it was. It's taken years to understand that I had witnessed the most coveted type of relationship on this great planet. I had witnessed and desired and was taken by their bond. In other words, I desired a bond. They had discovered something I had only heard about in songs. They had that thing that makes life worth living. I've always wanted that. I've always wanted to bond with someone. Now that I have what it takes to have a bond. ***I want the world to know that it's all about the companionship relationship, equally submitting bond.***

With a bond comes Freedom, acceptance, loyalty, and Love. A deep inner peace. The feeling that someone cares about you more than they can even express. You see it in their eyes, actions, and carefully chosen words of adoration towards each other. Who wouldn't want that???

But before we run off and start our search for our soulmate. There are some real issues that we have to address.

Are you capable of having a bond?

Are you willing to have a bond?

What are the steps to getting a bond?

How can you tell it's a bond?

How do you maintain a bond for life?

PUNISH THE ELEPHANT

www.ingramcontent.com/pod-product-compliance
Lightning Source LLC
LaVergne TN
LVHW081316060526
838201LV00005B/176